Vegetarian Chinese Cooking

STEP-BY-STEP

Vegetarian Chinese Cooking

WENDY LEE

||| •PARRAGON• |||

First published in Great Britain in 1995 by
Parragon Book Service Ltd
Unit 13-17
Avonbridge Trading Estate
Atlantic Road
Avonmouth
Bristol BS11 9QD

ISBN 1 85813 930 9

Produced by Haldane Mason, London

Printed in Italy

Acknowledgements:
Art Direction: Ron Samuels
Editor: Joanna Swinnerton
Series design: Pedro & Frances Pra-Lopez/Kingfisher Design
Page design: Anthony Limerick & Paul Pashby
Photography: Joff Lee
Styling: John Lee Studios
Home Economist: Wendy Lee

Photographs on pages 6, 18, 30, 46 and 62 are reproduced by permission of
ZEFA Picture Library UK Ltd.

Note:
*Cup measurements in this book are for American cups. Tablespoons are assumed to be 15 ml.
Unless otherwise stated, milk is assumed to be full-fat, eggs are standard size 2
and pepper is freshly ground black pepper.*

Contents

CHAPTER ONE

Appetizers

A selection of small portions of several different dishes usually starts the Chinese meal. The majority of these appetizers consist of tasty fillings enclosed in pastry-type wrappers which are fried until crisp. These are served with a simple dipping sauce of soy sauce, sherry and strips of spring onion (scallion) and chilli.

Snacks and appetizers are also sold at many roadside stalls throughout China, and are bought and eaten by people as they go about their daily tasks. After dusk, the pavements are filled with groups of families and friends cooking, eating and selling many delicious meals; this is an important part of their social lives, and is an enjoyable way of getting together and sharing their food.

Use the dishes in this section as appetizers to the main meal, or as snacks in their own right.

Opposite: *Hong Kong harbour shrouded in mist.*

STEP 1

STEP 2

STEP 3

STEP 4

CRISPY WONTONS WITH PIQUANT DIPPING SAUCE

Mushroom-filled crispy wontons are served on skewers with a dipping sauce flavoured with chillies.

SERVES 4

8 wooden skewers
1 tbsp vegetable oil
1 tbsp chopped onion
1 small garlic clove, chopped
$^1/_2$ tsp chopped ginger root
60 g/2 oz/$^1/_2$ cup flat mushrooms, chopped
16 wonton skins (see page 22)
vegetable oil for deep-frying
salt

SAUCE:
2 tbsp vegetable oil
2 spring onions (scallions), shredded thinly
1 red and 1 green chilli, deseeded and
    shredded thinly
3 tbsp light soy sauce
1 tbsp vinegar
1 tbsp dry sherry
pinch of sugar

1 Heat the oil in a wok or frying pan (skillet). Add the onion, garlic and ginger root, and stir-fry for 2 minutes. Stir in the mushrooms and fry for a further 2 minutes. Season well with salt and leave to cool.

2 Place 1 teaspoon of the cooled mushroom filling in the centre of each wonton skin. Bring two opposite corners together to cover the mixture and pinch together to seal. Repeat with the remaining corners.

3 Thread 2 wontons on to each skewer. Heat enough oil in a large saucepan to deep-fry the wontons in batches until golden and crisp. Remove with a perforated spoon and drain on paper towels.

4 To make the sauce, heat the oil in a small saucepan until quite hot, i.e. until a small cube of bread dropped in the oil browns in a few seconds. Put the spring onions (scallions) and chillies in a bowl and pour the hot oil slowly on top. Then mix in the remaining ingredients and serve with the crispy wontons.

HEATING THE OIL

Do not overheat the oil for deep-frying, or the wontons will brown on the outside before they are properly cooked inside.

8

STEP 2

STEP 3

STEP 4

STEP 5

CRISPY SEAWEED

Popular in many Chinese restaurants, this dish is served as a starter.
This 'seaweed' is in fact deep-fried spring greens.

SERVES 4

250 g/8 oz spring greens
vegetable oil for deep-frying
1 1/2 tsp caster (superfine) sugar
1 tsp salt
30 g/1 oz/1/4 cup flaked (slivered) almonds

1 Wash the spring greens thoroughly. Trim off the excess tough stalks. Place on paper towels or a dry tea towel (dish cloth) and leave to drain thoroughly.

2 Using a sharp knife, shred the spring greens finely and spread out on paper towels for about 30 minutes to dry.

3 Heat the oil in a wok or deep-fat fryer. Remove the pan from the heat and add the spring greens in batches. Return the pan to the heat and deep-fry until the greens begin to float to the surface and become translucent and crinkled. Remove the spring greens, using a perforated spoon, and drain on paper towels. Keep each batch warm.

4 Mix the sugar and salt together, sprinkle over the 'seaweed' and toss together to mix well.

5 Add the flaked (slivered) almonds to the hot oil and fry until lightly golden. Remove with a perforated spoon and drain on paper towels.

6 Serve the crispy 'seaweed' with the flaked (slivered) almonds.

TIME-SAVER

As a time-saver you can use a food processor to shred the greens finely.

Make sure you use only the best of the leaves; sort through the spring greens and discard any tough outer leaves, as these will spoil the overall taste and texture if they are included.

TOFU (BEANCURD) SANDWICHES

Slices of tofu (beancurd) are sandwiched together with a cucumber and cream cheese filling and coated in batter. Serve with a mint and yogurt dipping sauce.

STEP 2

MAKES 28

4 Chinese dried mushrooms (if unavailable, use thinly sliced open-cup mushrooms)
275 g/9 oz tofu (beancurd)
1/2 cucumber, grated
1 cm/1/2 inch piece ginger root, grated
60 g/2 oz/1/4 cup cream cheese
salt and pepper

BATTER:
125 g/4 oz/1 cup plain (all-purpose) flour
1 egg, beaten
120 ml/4 fl oz/1/2 cup water
1/2 tsp salt
2 tbsp sesame seeds
vegetable oil for deep-frying

SAUCE:
150 ml/1/4 pint/2/3 cup natural yogurt
2 tsp honey
2 tbsp chopped fresh mint

1 Place the dried mushrooms in a small bowl and cover with warm water. Leave to soak for 20–25 minutes. Drain and squeeze out the excess water. Remove the tough centres and chop the mushrooms.

2 Drain the tofu (beancurd) and slice thinly. Then cut each slice to make 2.5 cm/1 inch squares.

3 Squeeze the excess liquid from the cucumber and mix the cucumber with the mushrooms, grated ginger and cream cheese. Season well. Use as a filling to sandwich slices of tofu (beancurd) together to make about 28 sandwiches.

4 To make the batter, sift the flour into a bowl. Beat in the egg, water and salt to make a thick batter. Stir in the sesame seeds. Heat the oil in a large saucepan or wok. Coat the sandwiches in the batter and deep-fry in batches until golden. Remove with a perforated spoon and drain on paper towels.

5 To make the dipping sauce, blend together the yogurt, honey and mint. Serve with the tofu (beancurd) sandwiches.

> VARIATION
>
> For a change you could try using smoked tofu (beancurd), which will add extra flavour to the sandwiches.

STEP 3

STEP 4

STEP 4

STEP 2

STEP 3

STEP 4

STEP 5

SPRING ROLLS

Thin slices of vegetables are wrapped in pastry and deep-fried until crisp. Spring roll wrappers are available fresh or frozen from oriental suppliers and some supermarkets.

MAKES 12

5 Chinese dried mushrooms (if unavailable, use open-cup mushrooms)
1 large carrot
60 g/2 oz/1 cup canned bamboo shoots
2 spring onions (scallions)
60 g/2 oz Chinese leaves
2 tbsp vegetable oil
250 g/8 oz/4 cups bean-sprouts
1 tbsp soy sauce
12 spring roll wrappers
1 egg, beaten
vegetable oil for deep-frying
salt

1 Place the dried mushrooms in a small bowl and cover with warm water. Leave to soak for 20–25 minutes.

2 Drain the mushrooms and squeeze out the excess water. Remove the tough centres and slice the mushrooms thinly. Cut the carrot and bamboo shoots into very thin julienne strips. Chop the spring onions (scallions) and shred the Chinese leaves.

3 Heat the 2 tablespoons of oil in a wok or frying pan (skillet). Add the mushrooms, carrot and bamboo shoots, and stir-fry for 2 minutes. Add the spring

onions (scallions), Chinese leaves, bean-sprouts and soy sauce. Season with salt and stir-fry for 2 minutes. Leave to cool.

4 Divide the mixture into 12 equal portions and place one portion on the edge of each spring roll wrapper. Fold in the sides and roll each one up, brushing the join with a little beaten egg to seal.

5 Deep-fry the spring rolls in batches in hot oil in a wok or large saucepan for 4–5 minutes, or until golden and crispy. Take care that the oil is not too hot or the spring rolls will brown on the outside before cooking on the inside. Remove and drain on paper towels. Keep each batch warm while the others are being cooked. Serve at once.

SPRING ROLL WRAPPERS

If spring roll wrappers are unavailable, use sheets of filo pastry instead.

14

STEP 1

STEP 2

STEP 3

STEP 4

SWEET & SOUR CUCUMBER

Chunks of cucumber are marinated in vinegar and sweetened with honey to make a sweet and sour appetizer.

SERVES 4

1 cucumber
1 tsp salt
2 tsp honey
2 tbsp rice vinegar
3 tbsp chopped fresh coriander (cilantro)
2 tsp sesame oil
$^1/_4$ tsp crushed red peppercorns
strips of red and yellow (bell) pepper to
    garnish

1 Peel thin strips off the cucumber along the length. This gives a pretty striped effect. Cut the cucumber in quarters lengthways and then into 2.5 cm/1 inch long pieces. Place in a colander.

2 Sprinkle the salt over the cucumber and leave to rest for 30 minutes to allow the salt to draw out the excess water from the cucumber. Wash the cucumber thoroughly to remove the salt, drain and pat dry with paper towels.

3 Place the cucumber in a bowl. Combine the honey with the vinegar and pour over. Mix together and leave to marinate for 15 minutes.

4 Stir in the coriander (cilantro) and sesame oil, and place in a serving bowl.

5 Sprinkle over the crushed red peppercorns. Serve garnished with strips of red and yellow (bell) pepper.

RICE VINEGAR

Rice vinegar is a common Chinese cooking ingredient. White rice vinegar is made from rice wine, whereas red rice vinegar is made from fermented rice. Both have a distinctive flavour, but the white version tends to be used more often, as it will flavour but not colour all kinds of food. If rice vinegar is unavailable, use white wine vinegar instead.

CHAPTER TWO

Soups

In China soups are not usually served at the beginning of a meal but between courses to clear the palate. It is also quite common for Chinese families to have a large tureen of clear soup on the table which is served at the same time as the other dishes. Chinese cooks will often add some boiling clear stock or water to leftovers from the main course and serve it as an instant soup at the end of the meal.

Generally the soups are made from a good stock of vegetables, which are boiled for about 30 minutes before being strained, which gives a thin, clear broth. This can be served on its own, with a little soy sauce added for flavour. With the addition of a few suitable vegetables you can make a simple but tasty soup.

Most Chinese soups are of the thin, clear variety; however they do have a few thickened ones, such as the Hot & Sour Soup to which cornflour (cornstarch) is added. These soups can be eaten as a lunch or snack on their own.

Opposite: The familiar sight of a one-man 'taxi' in the backstreets of Hong Kong.

STEP 1

STEP 2

STEP 3

STEP 4

VEGETARIAN HOT & SOUR SOUP

This is a popular Chinese soup, which is unusual in that it is thickened. The characteristic 'hot' flavour is achieved by the addition of plenty of black pepper.

SERVES 4

4 Chinese dried mushrooms (if unavailable, use open-cup mushrooms)
125 g/4 oz firm tofu (beancurd)
60 g/2 oz/1 cup canned bamboo shoots
600 ml/1 pint/2½ cups vegetable stock or water
60 g/2 oz/⅓ cup peas
1 tbsp dark soy sauce
2 tbsp white wine vinegar
2 tbsp cornflour (cornstarch)
salt and pepper
sesame oil to serve

1 Place the Chinese dried mushrooms in a small bowl and cover with warm water. Leave to soak for 20–25 minutes.

2 Drain the mushrooms and squeeze out the excess water, reserving this. Remove the tough centres and cut the mushrooms into thin shreds. Shred the tofu (beancurd) and bamboo shoots.

3 Bring the stock or water to the boil in a large saucepan. Add the mushrooms, tofu (beancurd), bamboo shoots and peas. Simmer for 2 minutes.

4 Mix together the soy sauce, vinegar and cornflour (cornstarch) with 2 tablespoons of the reserved mushroom liquid. Stir into the soup with the remaining mushroom liquid. Bring to the boil and season with salt and plenty of pepper. Simmer for 2 minutes.

5 Serve in warmed bowls with a few drops of sesame oil in each.

MUSHROOMS

If you use open-cup mushrooms instead of dried mushrooms, add an extra 150 ml/¼ pint/⅔ cup vegetable stock or water to the soup, as these mushrooms do not need soaking.

STEP 1

STEP 2

STEP 3

STEP 4

WONTON SOUP

Spinach and pine kernel (nut) filled wontons are served in a clear soup. The recipe for the wonton skins makes 24 but the soup requires only half this quantity. The other half can be frozen ready for another time.

SERVES 4

WONTON SKINS:
1 egg
6 tbsp water
250 g/ 8 oz/ 2 cups plain (all-purpose)
   flour

FILLING:
125 g/ 4 oz/ ½ cup frozen chopped spinach,
   defrosted
15 g/ ½ oz/ 1 tbsp pine kernels (nuts),
   toasted and chopped
30 g/ 1 oz/ ¼ cup minced quorn (TVP)
salt

SOUP:
600 ml/ 1 pint/ 2½ cups vegetable stock
1 tbsp dry sherry
1 tbsp light soy sauce
2 spring onions (scallions), chopped

1 Beat the egg lightly in a bowl and mix with the water. Stir in the flour to form a stiff dough. Knead lightly, then cover with a damp cloth and leave to rest for 30 minutes.

2 Roll the dough out into a large sheet about 1.5 mm/ ¼ inch thick. Cut out 24 × 7 cm/3 inch squares. Dust each one lightly with flour. Only 12 squares are required for the soup so freeze the remainder.

3 To make the filling, squeeze out the excess water from the spinach. Mix the spinach with the pine kernels (nuts) and quorn (TVP). Season with salt.

4 Divide the mixture into 12 equal portions and place one portion in the centre of each square. Seal by bringing the opposite corners of each square together and squeezing well.

5 To make the soup, bring the stock, sherry and soy sauce to the boil, add the wontons and boil rapidly for 2–3 minutes. Add the spring onions (scallions) and serve in warmed bowls immediately.

FREEZING WONTON WRAPPERS

To freeze the leftover wonton skins, place small squares of baking parchment in between each skin, then place in a freezer bag and freeze. Defrost thoroughly before using.

SWEETCORN & LENTIL SOUP

This pale-coloured soup is made with sweetcorn and green lentils, and is similar in style to the traditional crab and sweetcorn soup.

SERVES 4

30 g/1 oz/2 tbsp green lentils
1 litre/1 ¾ pints/4 cups vegetable stock
1 cm/½ inch piece ginger root, chopped
 finely
2 tsp soy sauce
1 tsp sugar
1 tbsp cornflour (cornstarch)
3 tbsp dry sherry
325 g/11 oz can of sweetcorn
1 egg white
1 tsp sesame oil
salt and pepper

TO GARNISH:
strips spring onion (scallion)
strips red chilli

1 Wash the lentils in a sieve (strainer). Place in a saucepan with the stock, ginger root, soy sauce and sugar. Bring to the boil and boil rapidly, uncovered, for 10 minutes. Skim off any froth on the surface. Reduce the heat, cover and simmer for 15 minutes.

2 Mix the cornflour (cornstarch) with the sherry in a small bowl. Add the sweetcorn with the liquid from the can and cornflour (cornstarch) mix to the saucepan. Simmer for 2 minutes.

3 Whisk the egg white lightly with the sesame oil. Pour the egg mixture into the soup in a thin stream, remove from the heat and stir. The egg white will form white strands.

4 Season to taste. Pour into 4 warmed soup bowls and garnish with strips of spring onion (scallion) and chilli before serving.

STEP 2

USING CANNED LENTILS

As a time-saver use a 425 g/14 oz can of green lentils instead of dried ones. Place the lentils and sweetcorn together in a large saucepan with the stock and flavourings, bring to the boil and simmer for 2 minutes, then continue the recipe from step 2 as above. There is no need to boil canned lentils rapidly for 10 minutes.

STEP 3

STEP 3

25

STEP 1

STEP 3

STEP 4

STEP 5

MUSHROOM & CUCUMBER NOODLE SOUP

A light, refreshing clear soup of mushrooms, cucumber and small pieces of rice noodles, flavoured with soy sauce and a touch of garlic.

SERVES 4

*125 g/4 oz flat or open-cup mushrooms
1/2 cucumber
2 spring onions (scallions)
1 garlic clove
2 tbsp vegetable oil
30 g/1 oz/1/4 cup Chinese rice noodles
3/4 tsp salt
1 tbsp soy sauce*

1 Wash the mushrooms and slice thinly. Do not remove the peel as this adds more flavour. Halve the cucumber lengthways. Scoop out the seeds, using a teaspoon, and slice the cucumber thinly.

2 Chop the spring onions (scallions) finely and cut the garlic clove into thin strips.

3 Heat the oil in a large saucepan or wok. Add the spring onions (scallions) and garlic, and stir-fry for 30 seconds. Add the mushrooms and stir-fry for 2–3 minutes.

4 Stir in 600 ml/1 pint/2 1/2 cups water. Break the noodles into short lengths and add to the soup. Bring to the boil.

5 Add the cucumber slices, salt and soy sauce, and simmer for 2–3 minutes.

6 Serve the soup in warmed bowls, distributing the noodles and vegetables evenly.

CUCUMBER SEEDS

Scooping the seeds out from the cucumber gives it a prettier effect when sliced, and also helps to reduce any bitterness, but if you prefer, you can leave them in.

STEP 1

STEP 2

STEP 3

STEP 4

LETTUCE & TOFU (BEANCURD) SOUP

This is a delicate, clear soup of shredded lettuce and small chunks of tofu (beancurd) with sliced carrot and spring onion (scallion).

SERVES 4

200 g/7 oz tofu (beancurd)
2 tbsp vegetable oil
1 carrot, sliced thinly
1 cm/¹/₂ inch piece ginger root, cut into thin shreds
3 spring onions (scallions), sliced diagonally
1.25 litres/2 pints/5 cups vegetable stock
2 tbsp soy sauce
2 tbsp dry sherry
1 tsp sugar
125 g/4 oz/1¹/₂ cups cos (romaine) lettuce, shredded
salt and pepper

1 Cut the tofu (beancurd) into small cubes. Heat the oil in a wok or large saucepan, add the tofu (beancurd) and stir-fry until browned. Remove with a perforated spoon and drain on paper towels.

2 Add the carrot, ginger root and spring onions (scallions) to the wok or saucepan and stir-fry for 2 minutes.

3 Add the stock, soy sauce, sherry and sugar. Bring to the boil and simmer for 1 minute.

4 Add the lettuce and stir until it has just wilted.

5 Return the tofu (beancurd) to the pan to reheat. Season with salt and pepper and serve in warmed bowls.

DECORATIVE CARROTS

For a prettier effect, score grooves along the length of the carrot with a sharp knife before slicing. This will create a flower effect as the carrot is cut into rounds. You could also try slicing the carrot on the diagonal to make longer slices. Try garnishing the soup with carrot curls – very fine strips of carrot that have been placed in iced water to make them curl up.

CHAPTER THREE

Main Meals

An abundance of high-quality produce can be bought from the markets in the towns and villages of China, and fresh food is purchased daily by endless streams of people buying the freshest goods for their family meals.

The simplest meal has a central dish of rice or noodles with a stir-fry or steamed dumplings all of which are served at the same time, quite different from our Western way of eating. When entertaining, choose several different dishes to give as much variety of taste as possible, and prepare as much as you can in advance to enable you to spend more time with your guests than in the kitchen.

The following recipes contain ingredients that blend together to achieve a balanced contrast in colour, flavour and texture. They are quick to prepare and cook. All the recipes in this section may be served as main courses with an accompaniment of rice or noodles.

Opposite: *One of the great wonders of the world – the Great Wall of China.*

STEP 1

STEP 3

STEP 4

STEP 5

VEGETABLE & NUT STIR-FRY

*A colourful selection of vegetables are stir-fried in a creamy peanut
sauce and sprinkled with nuts to serve.*

SERVES 4

3 tbsp crunchy peanut butter
150 ml/¼ pint/⅔ cup water
1 tbsp soy sauce
1 tsp sugar
1 carrot
½ red onion
4 baby courgettes (zucchini)
1 red (bell) pepper
250 g/8 oz egg thread noodles
30 g/1 oz/¼ cup peanuts, chopped roughly
2 tbsp vegetable oil
1 tsp sesame oil
1 small green chilli, deseeded and sliced
    thinly
1 garlic clove, sliced thinly
225 g/7½ oz can of water chestnuts,
    drained and sliced
175 g/6 oz/3 cups bean-sprouts
salt

1 Blend the peanut butter with the
water gradually in a small bowl.
Stir in the soy sauce and sugar.

2 Cut the carrot into thin
matchsticks and slice the onion.
Slice the courgettes (zucchini) on the
diagonal and cut the (bell) pepper into
chunks.

3 Bring a large pan of water to the
boil and add the egg noodles.
Remove from the heat immediately and
leave to rest for 4 minutes, stirring
occasionally to divide the noodles.

4 Heat a wok or large frying pan
(skillet), add the peanuts and dry-
fry until they are beginning to brown.
Remove and set aside.

5 Add the oils to the pan and heat.
Add the carrot, onion, courgette
(zucchini), (bell) pepper, chilli and garlic,
and stir-fry for 2–3 minutes. Add the
water chestnuts, bean-sprouts and
peanut sauce. Bring to the boil and heat
thoroughly. Season to taste. Drain the
noodles and serve with the stir-fry.
Sprinkle with the peanuts.

VARIATION

The vegetables in this dish can be varied
according to your taste and their
availability. Make sure you choose a
variety of colours for the best effect.

STEP 1

STEP 2

STEP 3

STEP 4

AUBERGINES (EGGPLANTS) IN BLACK BEAN SAUCE

Stir-fried aubergine (eggplant) is served in a black bean sauce with garlic and spring onions (scallions). This would go well with rice and another vegetable dish such as stir-fried baby corn and green beans.

SERVES 4

60 g/2 oz/generous ⅓ cup dried black beans
450 ml/¾ pint/scant 2 cups vegetable
    stock
1 tbsp malt vinegar
1 tbsp dry sherry
1 tbsp soy sauce
1 tbsp sugar
1½ tsp cornflour (cornstarch)
1 red chilli, deseeded and chopped
1 cm/½ inch piece ginger root, chopped
2 aubergines (eggplants)
2 tsp salt
3 tbsp vegetable oil
2 garlic cloves, sliced
4 spring onions (scallions), cut diagonally
shredded radishes to garnish

1 Soak the beans overnight in plenty of cold water. Drain and place in a saucepan. Cover with cold water, bring to the boil and boil rapidly, uncovered, for 10 minutes. Drain. Return the beans to the saucepan with the stock and bring to the boil.

2 Blend together the vinegar, sherry, soy sauce, sugar, cornflour (cornstarch), chilli and ginger in a small bowl. Add to the saucepan, cover and simmer for 40 minutes, or until the

beans are tender and the sauce has thickened. Stir occasionally.

3 Cut the aubergines (eggplants) into chunks and place in a colander. Sprinkle over the salt and leave to drain for 30 minutes. Rinse well to remove the salt and dry on paper towels.

4 Heat the oil in a wok or large frying pan (skillet). Add the aubergine (eggplant) and garlic. Stir-fry for 3–4 minutes until the aubergine (eggplant) has started to brown.

5 Add the sauce to the aubergine (eggplant) with the spring onions (scallions). Heat thoroughly and garnish with radish shreds.

TIME-SAVER

To save time, you can use a ready-made black bean sauce instead of making your own. You will need to use about 6 tablespoonfuls.

STIR-FRIED MUSHROOMS, CUCUMBER & SMOKED TOFU (BEANCURD)

Chunks of cucumber and smoked tofu (beancurd) stir-fried with straw mushrooms, mangetout (snow peas) and corn in a yellow bean sauce.

STEP 1

SERVES 4

1 large cucumber
1 tsp salt
225 g/7½ oz smoked tofu (beancurd)
2 tbsp vegetable oil
60 g/2 oz mangetout (snow peas)
125 g/4 oz/8 baby corn
1 celery stick, sliced diagonally
425 g/14 oz can of straw mushrooms,
    drained
2 spring onions (scallions), cut into strips
1 cm/½ inch piece ginger root, chopped
1 tbsp yellow bean sauce
1 tbsp light soy sauce
1 tbsp dry sherry

1 Halve the cucumber lengthways. Remove the seeds, using a teaspoon. Cut into cubes, place in a colander and sprinkle over the salt. Leave to drain for 10 minutes. Rinse thoroughly in cold water to remove the salt and drain thoroughly.

2 Cut the tofu (beancurd) into cubes. Heat the oil in a wok or large frying pan (skillet). Add the tofu (beancurd), mangetout (snow peas), baby corn and celery. Stir until the tofu (beancurd) is lightly browned.

3 Add the straw mushrooms, spring onions (scallions) and ginger, and stir-fry for a further minute.

4 Stir in the cucumber, yellow bean sauce, soy sauce, sherry and 2 tablespoons of water.

5 Stir-fry for 1 minute before serving.

STEP 2

STEP 3

STRAW MUSHROOMS

Straw mushrooms are available in cans from oriental suppliers and some supermarkets. If unavailable, substitute 250 g/8 oz baby button mushrooms.

STEP 4

STEP 2

STEP 3

STEP 4

STEP 6

VEGETABLE CASSEROLE WITH BLACK BEANS

This colourful Chinese-style casserole is made with tofu (beancurd), vegetables and black bean sauce.

SERVES 4

6 Chinese dried mushrooms (if unavailable,
   use thinly sliced open-cup mushrooms)
275 g/9 oz tofu (beancurd)
3 tbsp vegetable oil
1 carrot, cut into thin strips
125 g/4 oz mangetout (snow peas)
125 g/4 oz/8 baby corn, halved lengthways
225 g/7½ oz can of sliced bamboo shoots,
   drained
1 red (bell) pepper, cut into chunks
125 g/4 oz/1½ cups Chinese leaves,
   shredded
1 tbsp soy sauce
1 tbsp black bean sauce
1 tsp sugar
1 tsp cornflour (cornstarch)
vegetable oil for deep-frying
250 g/8 oz Chinese rice noodles
salt

1 Place the Chinese dried mushrooms in a small bowl and cover with warm water. Leave to soak for 20–25 minutes. Drain and squeeze out the excess water, reserving the liquid. Remove the tough centres and slice the mushrooms thinly.

2 Cut the tofu (beancurd) into cubes. Boil in a saucepan of lightly salted water for 2–3 minutes to firm up. Drain thoroughly.

3 Heat half the oil in a large flameproof casserole or saucepan. Add the tofu (beancurd) and fry until lightly browned all over. Remove with a perforated spoon and drain on paper towels.

4 Add the remaining oil and stir-fry the mushrooms, carrot, mangetout (snow peas), baby corn, bamboo shoots and (bell) pepper for 2–3 minutes. Add the Chinese leaves and tofu (beancurd), and stir-fry for a further 2 minutes.

5 Stir in the soy sauce, black bean sauce and sugar, and season with salt. Add 6 tablespoons of the reserved mushroom liquid (or water if you are using ordinary mushrooms), mixed with cornflour (cornstarch).

6 Bring to the boil, reduce the heat, cover and braise for 2–3 minutes until the sauce has thickened slightly. Heat the oil for deep-frying in a large saucepan. Add the noodles in batches and deep-fry until puffed up and lightly golden. Drain on paper towels and serve with the casserole.

STEP 2

STEP 5

STEP 5

STEP 6

MONEY BAGS

These traditional steamed dumplings are made with a mushroom and sweetcorn filling. Eat them as they are, or try dipping them in a mixture of soy sauce, sherry and slivers of ginger root.

SERVES 4

3 Chinese dried mushrooms (if unavailable, use thinly sliced open-cup mushrooms)
250 g/ 8 oz/ 2 cups plain (all-purpose) flour
1 egg, beaten
75 ml/ 3 fl oz/¹/₃ cup water
1 tsp baking powder
³/₄ tsp salt
2 tbsp vegetable oil
2 spring onions (scallions), chopped
90 g/ 3 oz/¹/₂ cup sweetcorn kernels
¹/₂ red chilli, deseeded and chopped
1 tbsp brown bean sauce

1 Place the dried mushrooms in a small bowl, cover with warm water and leave to soak for 20–25 minutes.

2 To make the wrappers, sift the flour into a bowl. Add the egg and mix in lightly. Stir in the water, baking powder and salt. Mix to make a soft dough. Knead lightly until smooth on a floured board. Cover with a damp cloth and set aside for 5–6 minutes. This allows the baking powder time to activate, so that the dumplings swell when steaming.

3 Drain the mushrooms, squeezing them dry. Remove the tough centres and chop the mushrooms.

4 Heat the oil in a wok or large frying pan (skillet) and stir-fry the mushrooms, spring onions (scallions), sweetcorn and chilli for 2 minutes. Stir in the brown bean sauce and remove from the heat.

5 Roll the dough into a large sausage and cut into 24 even-sized pieces. Roll each piece out into a thin round and place a teaspoonful of the filling in the centre. Gather up the edges to a point, pinch together and twist to seal.

6 Stand the dumplings in an oiled steaming basket. Place over a saucepan of simmering water, cover and steam for 12–14 minutes before serving.

COOKING WITH CABBAGE LEAVES

For extra flavour and to help to prevent the dumplings falling through the steamer, place them on cabbage leaves inside the steamer.

CARROTS & PARSNIPS WITH COCONUT

Sliced carrots and chunks of parsnip are cooked in a creamy coconut sauce with ground almonds and served on a bed of spinach.

STEP 1

SERVES 2

90 g/ 3 oz/¹⁄₃ cup creamed coconut
300 ml/¹⁄₂ pint/ 1¹⁄₄ cups hot water
15 g/¹⁄₂ oz/ 2 tbsp flaked (slivered) almonds
4 tbsp vegetable oil
5 cardamom pods
4 thin slices ginger root
350 g/12 oz/2¹⁄₂ cups carrots, sliced
350 g/12 oz/2¹⁄₂ cups parsnips, cut into
*   small chunks*
¹⁄₄ tsp five-spice powder
15 g/¹⁄₂ oz/2 tbsp ground almonds
200 g/7 oz/4 cups young spinach leaves
¹⁄₂ red onion, sliced thinly
1 garlic clove, sliced
salt

1 Crumble the creamed coconut into a bowl or jug, add the hot water and stir until dissolved.

2 Heat a saucepan and dry-fry the flaked (slivered) almonds until golden. Remove and set aside.

3 Heat half the oil in the saucepan. Add the cardamom pods and ginger root. Fry for 30 seconds to flavour the oil. Add the carrots and parsnips. Stir-fry for 2–3 minutes.

4 Stir in the five-spice powder and ground almonds, and pour in the coconut liquid. Bring to the boil and season with salt to taste. Cover and simmer for 12–15 minutes until the vegetables are tender. Stir occasionally, adding extra water if necessary.

5 Wash the spinach and drain thoroughly. Remove any stalks. Heat the remaining oil in a wok or large frying pan (skillet). Add the onion and garlic, and stir-fry for 2 minutes. Add the spinach and stir-fry until it has just wilted. Drain off any excess liquid formed. Season with salt.

6 Remove the cardamom pods and ginger root from the carrots and parsnips, and adjust the seasoning. Serve on a bed of the spinach sprinkled with the almonds.

CARDAMOM

Lightly crush the cardamom pods before using, as this helps to release their flavour.

STEP 3

STEP 4

STEP 5

STEP 1

STEP 2

STEP 4

STEP 5

LENTIL BALLS WITH SWEET & SOUR SAUCE

Crisp golden lentil balls are served in a sweet and sour sauce with (bell) peppers and pineapple chunks.

SERVES 4

250 g/8 oz/1 cup red lentils
450 ml/¾ pint/scant 2 cups water
½ green chilli, deseeded and chopped
4 spring onions (scallions), chopped finely
1 garlic clove, crushed
1 tsp salt
4 tbsp pineapple juice from can
1 egg, beaten
vegetable oil for deep-frying

SAUCE:
3 tbsp white wine vinegar
2 tbsp sugar
2 tbsp tomato purée (paste)
1 tsp sesame oil
1 tsp cornflour (cornstarch)
½ tsp salt
6 tbsp water
2 canned pineapple rings
2 tbsp vegetable oil
½ red (bell) pepper, cut into chunks
½ green (bell) pepper, cut into chunks

1 Wash the lentils, then place in a saucepan with the water and bring to the boil. Skim and boil rapidly for 10 minutes, uncovered. Reduce the heat and simmer for 5 minutes until you have a fairly dry mixture. Considerably less water is used to cook these lentils than is normally required, so take care they do not burn as they cook. Stir occasionally.

2 Remove from the heat and stir in the chilli, spring onions (scallions), garlic, salt and pineapple juice. Leave to cool for 10 minutes.

3 To make the sauce, mix together the vinegar, sugar, tomato purée (paste) sesame oil, cornflour (cornstarch), salt and water, and set aside. Cut the pineapple into chunks.

4 Add the beaten egg to the lentil mixture. Heat the oil in a large saucepan or wok and deep-fry tablespoonfuls of the mixture in batches until crisp and golden. Remove with a perforated spoon and drain on paper towels.

5 Heat the 2 tablespoons oil in a wok or frying pan (skillet). Stir-fry the (bell) peppers for 2 minutes. Add the sauce mixture with the pineapple chunks. Bring to the boil, then reduce the heat and simmer for 1 minute, stirring constantly, until the sauce has thickened. Add the lentil balls and heat thoroughly, taking care not to break them up. Serve with rice or noodles.

CHAPTER FOUR

Vegetables & Salads

Due to the vast size of China, in which there are many different climates, the country produces a huge variety of vegetables. These play a significant role in the Chinese diet, and are considered important in their own right rather than as mere accompaniments.

Many Westerners overcook their vegetables, boiling them in too much water and causing them to lose all their flavour and colour as well as their valuable vitamins and minerals. Stir-frying was until recently a method of cooking unique to the Chinese. The raw ingredients are cooked quickly with a minimum of oil or water over a high heat. This ensures that flavours, colours and nutrients are preserved leaving the vegetables crisp and colourful.

A mixture of raw and cooked vegetables is often used in Chinese salads, and these are picked fresh as they are needed. Choose firm crisp vegetables and cook them while they are at their best, as this will make all the difference to your final dish.

Opposite: A tempting array of fresh fruits and vegetables in the western district of Hong Kong.

STEP 1

STEP 2

STEP 4

STEP 5

AUBERGINES (EGGPLANTS) IN CHILLI SAUCE

Strips of aubergine (eggplant) are deep-fried, then served in a fragrant chilli sauce with carrot matchsticks and spring onions (scallions).

SERVES 4

1 large aubergine (eggplant)
vegetable oil for deep-frying
2 carrots
4 spring onions (scallions)
2 large garlic cloves
1 tbsp vegetable oil
2 tsp chilli sauce
1 tbsp soy sauce
1 tbsp dry sherry

1 Slice the aubergine (eggplant) and then cut into strips about the size of potato chips (French fries).

2 Heat enough oil in a large heavy-based saucepan to deep-fry the aubergine (eggplant) in batches until just browned. Remove the strips with a perforated spoon and drain them on paper towels.

3 Cut the carrots into thin matchsticks. Trim and slice the spring onions (scallions) diagonally. Slice the garlic cloves.

4 Heat 1 tablespoon of oil in a wok or large frying pan (skillet). Add the carrot matchsticks and stir-fry for 1 minute; then add the chopped spring onions (scallions) and garlic and stir-fry for a further minute.

5 Stir in the chilli sauce, soy sauce and sherry, then stir in the drained aubergine (eggplant). Mix well to ensure that the vegetables are heated through thoroughly before serving.

MILDER FLAVOUR

For a milder dish, substitute hoisin sauce for the chilli sauce. This can be bought ready-made from all supermarkets.

STEP 1

STEP 2

STEP 3

STEP 4

GINGERED BROCCOLI WITH ORANGE

Thinly sliced broccoli florets are lightly stir-fried and served in a ginger and orange sauce.

SERVES 4

750 g/1½ lb broccoli
2 thin slices ginger root
2 garlic cloves
1 orange
2 tsp cornflour (cornstarch)
1 tbsp light soy sauce
½ tsp sugar
2 tbsp vegetable oil

1 Divide the broccoli into small florets. Peel the stems, using a vegetable peeler, and then cut the stems into thin slices. Cut the ginger root into matchsticks and slice the garlic.

2 Peel 2 long strips of zest from the orange and cut into thin strips. Place the strips in a bowl, cover with cold water and set aside. Squeeze the juice from the orange and mix with the cornflour (cornstarch), soy sauce, sugar and 4 tablespoons water.

3 Heat the oil in a wok or large frying pan (skillet). Add the broccoli stem slices and stir-fry for 2 minutes. Add the ginger root slices, garlic and broccoli florets, and stir-fry for a further 3 minutes.

4 Stir in the orange sauce mixture and cook, stirring constantly, until the sauce has thickened and coated the broccoli.

5 Drain the reserved orange rind and stir in before serving.

VARIATION

This dish could be made with cauliflower, if you prefer, or a mixture of cauliflower and broccoli.

LEMON CHINESE LEAVES

These stir-fried Chinese leaves are served with a tangy sauce made of grated lemon rind, lemon juice and ginger.

STEP 1

SERVES 4

500 g/1 lb Chinese leaves
3 tbsp vegetable oil
1 cm/½ inch piece ginger root, grated
1 tsp salt
1 tsp sugar
120 ml/4 fl oz/½ cup water or vegetable stock
1 tsp grated lemon rind
1 tbsp cornflour (cornstarch)
1 tbsp lemon juice

1 Separate the Chinese leaves, wash and drain thoroughly. Pat dry with paper towels. Cut into 5 cm/2 inch wide slices.

2 Heat the oil in a wok or large frying pan (skillet). Add the grated ginger root, followed by the Chinese leaves, stir-fry for 2–3 minutes or until the leaves begin to wilt. Add the salt and sugar, and mix well until the leaves soften. Remove the leaves with a perforated spoon and set aside.

3 Add the water or vegetable stock to the pan with the grated lemon zest and bring to the boil. Meanwhile, mix the cornflour (cornstarch) to a smooth paste with the lemon juice, then add to the

water or stock in the pan. Simmer, stirring constantly, for about 1 minute to make a smooth sauce.

4 Return the cooked leaves to the pan and mix thoroughly. Arrange on a serving plate and serve immediately.

STEP 2

STEP 3

CHINESE LEAVES

If Chinese leaves are unavailable, substitute slices of savoy cabbage. Cook for 1 extra minute to soften the leaves.

STEP 4

STEP 1

STEP 2

STEP 3

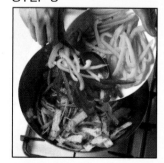

STEP 4

GOLDEN NEEDLES WITH BAMBOO SHOOTS

Golden needles are the dried flower buds of the tiger lily. They are usually sold in the dried form and can be obtained from specialist Chinese shops. They give a unique musky flavour to this dish.

SERVES 4

30 g/ 1 oz/ ¼ cup dried lily flowers
2 × 225 g/ 7½ oz cans of bamboo shoots, drained
60 g/ 2 oz/ ½ cup cornflour (cornstarch)
vegetable oil for deep-frying
1 tbsp vegetable oil
450ml/ ¾ pint/ scant 2 cups vegetable stock
1 tbsp dark soy sauce
1 tbsp dry sherry
1 tsp sugar
1 large garlic clove, sliced
½ each red, green and yellow (bell) peppers

1 Soak the lily flowers in hot water for 30 minutes.

2 Coat the bamboo shoots in cornflour (cornstarch). Heat enough oil in a large heavy-based saucepan to deep-fry the bamboo shoots in batches until just beginning to colour. Remove with a perforated spoon and drain on paper towels.

3 Drain the lily flowers and trim off the hard ends. Heat 1 tablespoon oil in a wok or large frying pan (skillet). Add the lily flowers, bamboo shoots, stock, soy sauce, sherry, sugar and garlic.

4 Slice the (bell) peppers thinly and add to the pan. Bring to the boil, stirring constantly, then reduce the heat and simmer for 5 minutes. Add extra water or stock if necessary.

COATING THE BAMBOO SHOOTS

To coat the bamboo shoots easily with cornflour (cornstarch), place the cornflour (cornstarch) in a plastic bag, add the bamboo shoots in batches and shake well.

STEP 1

STEP 3

STEP 4

STEP 5

SPINACH WITH STRAW MUSHROOMS

Straw mushrooms are available in cans from oriental shops. Here they are served with spinach, raisins and pine kernels (nuts). You can use button mushrooms instead, if straw mushrooms are unavailable.

SERVES 4

30 g/1 oz/¼ cup pine kernels (nuts)
500 g/1 lb fresh spinach leaves
3 tbsp vegetable oil
1 red onion, sliced
2 garlic cloves, sliced
425 g/14 oz can of straw mushrooms,
    drained
30 g/1 oz/3 tbsp raisins
2 tbsp soy sauce
salt

1 Heat a wok or large frying pan (skillet) and dry-fry the pine kernels (nuts) until lightly browned. Remove and set aside.

2 Wash the spinach thoroughly, picking the leaves over and removing long stalks. Drain and pat dry with paper towels.

3 Heat the oil in the wok or frying pan (skillet). Add the onion and garlic, and stir-fry for 1 minute.

4 Add the spinach and mushrooms, and continue to stir-fry until the leaves have wilted. Drain off any excess liquid.

5 Stir in the raisins, reserved pine kernels (nuts) and soy sauce. Stir-fry until thoroughly heated and well-mixed. Season to taste with salt before serving.

ADDING FLAVOUR

Soak the raisins in 2 tablespoons dry sherry before using. This helps to plump them up as well as adding extra flavour to the stir-fry.

GADO GADO SALAD

This salad is a mixture of cooked and raw vegetables in a spicy peanut dressing. The vegetables can either be arranged in individual piles on the serving platter or mixed together.

STEP 2

SERVES 4

250 g/8 oz new potatoes, scrubbed
125 g/4 oz green beans
125 g/4 oz cauliflower, broken into small
  florets
125 g/4 oz/1 ½ cups white cabbage,
  shredded
1 carrot, cut into thin sticks
¼ cucumber, cut into chunks
125 g/4 oz/2 cups bean-sprouts
2 hard-boiled (hard-cooked) eggs

SAUCE:
6 tbsp crunchy peanut butter
300 ml/½ pint/1 ¼ cups cold water
1 garlic clove, crushed
1 fresh red chilli, deseeded and finely
  chopped
2 tbsp soy sauce
1 tbsp dry sherry
2 tsp sugar
1 tbsp lemon juice

1 Halve the potatoes and place in a saucepan of lightly salted water. Bring to the boil and then simmer for 12–15 minutes, or until cooked through. Drain and plunge into cold water to cool.

2 Bring another pan of lightly salted water to the boil. Add the green

STEP 3

beans, cauliflower and cabbage, and cook for 3 minutes. Drain and plunge the vegetables into cold water to cool and prevent any further cooking.

3 Drain the potatoes and other cooked vegetables. Arrange in piles on a large serving platter with the carrot, cucumber and bean-sprouts.

4 Remove the shells from the hard-boiled (hard-cooked) eggs, cut into quarters and arrange on the salad. Cover and set aside.

STEP 4

5 To make the sauce, place the peanut butter in a bowl and blend in the water gradually, followed by the remaining ingredients.

6 Uncover the salad, place the sauce in a separate serving bowl and drizzle some over each serving.

COCONUT MILK

For extra flavour to the peanut sauce, use coconut milk instead of water. This can be purchased from specialist oriental shops and some supermarkets.

STEP 5

STEP 1

STEP 2

STEP 3

STEP 4

ORIENTAL SALAD

This colourful crisp salad has a fresh orange dressing and is topped with crunchy vermicelli.

SERVES 4–6

30 g/1 oz/¼ cup dried vermicelli
½ head Chinese leaves
125 g/4 oz/2 cups bean-sprouts
6 radishes
125 g/4 oz mangetout (snow peas)
1 large carrot
125 g/4 oz sprouting beans

DRESSING:
juice of 1 orange
1 tbsp sesame seeds, toasted
1 tsp honey
1 tsp sesame oil
1 tbsp hazelnut oil

1 Break the vermicelli into small strands. Heat a wok or frying pan (skillet) and dry-fry the vermicelli until lightly golden. Remove from the pan and set aside.

2 Shred the Chinese leaves and wash with the bean-sprouts. Drain thoroughly and place in a large bowl. Slice the radishes. Trim the mangetout (snow peas) and cut each into 3. Cut the carrot into thin matchsticks. Add the sprouting beans and prepared vegetables to the bowl.

3 Place all the dressing ingredients in a screw-top jar and shake until well-blended. Pour over the salad and toss.

4 Transfer the salad to a serving bowl and sprinkle over the reserved vermicelli before serving.

SPROUTING BEANS

If you are unable to buy sprouting beans, you can make your own. Use a mixture of mung and aduki beans and chick-peas (garbanzo beans). Soak the beans overnight in cold water, drain and rinse. Place in a large glass jam jar and cover the mouth of the jar with a piece of muslin tied on to secure it. Lay the jar on its side and place in indirect light. For the next 2–3 days rinse the beans once each day in cold water until they are ready to eat.

CHAPTER FIVE

Rice & Noodles

Rice and noodles form the central part of most oriental meals, particularly in the southern part of China. In the north the staple foods tend to contain more wheat-based products, such as dumplings. Rice and noodles supply the carbohydrate necessary for a nutritious meal, and though bland in themselves they provide a complementary texture to the other ingredients and absorb the stronger flavours of other dishes, making them an essential and very satisfying part of the Chinese meal.

The most common types of rice used in Chinese cuisine include white or brown long-grain rice and glutinous rice. The shorter grain of the glutinous rice has a slight stickiness when cooked, which makes it ideal for eating with chopsticks.

Rice can be boiled and then steamed, or it can be fried with other ingredients added, such as scrambled eggs, spring onions (scallions) or peas, then flavoured with soy sauce. It is also used to make wines, vinegars, noodles and flour, which makes it a very important ingredient.

A wide variety of Chinese noodles are available, made from wheat, buckwheat or rice flours. Like rice, they are very versatile; they can be boiled or fried, and served plain with a sauce, or in a soup.

Opposite: *A 1000-year old banyan tree overhangs a rice field in the Guangxi province.*

HOMEMADE NOODLES WITH STIR-FRIED VEGETABLES

These noodles are simple to make; you do not need a pasta-making machine as they are rolled out by hand.

STEP 1

STEP 3

STEP 4

STEP 5

SERVES 2–4

NOODLES:
125 g/4 oz/1 cup plain (all-purpose) flour
2 tbsp cornflour (cornstarch)
½ tsp salt
120 ml/4 fl oz/½ cup boiling water
5 tbsp vegetable oil

STIR-FRY:
1 courgette (zucchini)
1 celery stick
1 carrot
125 g/4 oz open-cup mushrooms
1 leek
125 g/4 oz broccoli
125 g/4 oz/2 cups bean-sprouts
1 tbsp soy sauce
2 tsp rice wine vinegar (if unavailable, use
   white wine vinegar)
½ tsp sugar

1 To prepare the noodles, sift the flour, cornflour (cornstarch) and salt into a bowl. Make a well in the centre and pour in the boiling water and 1 teaspoon of the oil. Mix quickly, using a wooden spoon, to make a soft dough. Cover and leave for 5–6 minutes.

2 Prepare the vegetables for the stir-fry. Cut the courgette (zucchini),

celery and carrot into thin sticks. Slice the mushrooms and leek. Divide the broccoli into small florets, peel and thinly slice the stalks.

3 Make the noodles by breaking off small pieces of dough and rolling into balls. Then roll each ball across a very lightly oiled work surface (counter) with the palm of your hand to form thin noodles. Do not worry if some of the noodles break into shorter lengths. Set the noodles aside.

4 Heat 3 tablespoons of oil in a wok or large frying pan (skillet). Add the noodles in batches and fry over a high heat for 1 minute. Reduce the heat and cook for a further 2 minutes. Remove and drain on paper towels. Set aside.

5 Heat the remaining oil in the pan. Add the courgette (zucchini), celery and carrot, and stir-fry for 1 minute. Add the mushrooms, broccoli and leek, and stir-fry for a further minute. Stir in the remaining ingredients and mix well until thoroughly heated.

6 Add the noodles and toss to mix together over a high heat. Serve immediately.

STEP 2

STEP 3

STEP 4

STEP 5

CHOW MEIN

Egg noodles are fried with a colourful variety of vegetables to make this well-known dish.

SERVES 4

500 g / 1 lb egg noodles
4 tbsp vegetable oil
1 onion, sliced thinly
2 carrots, cut into thin sticks
125 g/4 oz/1¹/₃ cups button mushrooms,
    quartered
125 g/4 oz mangetout (snow peas)
¹/₂ cucumber, cut into sticks
125 g/4 oz/2 cups spinach, shredded
125 g/4 oz/2 cups bean-sprouts
2 tbsp dark soy sauce
1 tbsp sherry
1 tsp salt
1 tsp sugar
1 tsp cornflour (cornstarch)
1 tsp sesame oil

1 Cook the noodles according to the packet instructions. Drain and rinse under running cold water until cool. Set aside.

2 Heat 3 tablespoons of the vegetable oil in a wok or large frying pan (skillet). Add the onion and carrots, and stir-fry for 1 minute. Add the mushrooms, mangetout (snow peas) and cucumber, and stir-fry for a further minute.

3 Stir in the remaining vegetable oil and add the drained noodles with the spinach and bean-sprouts.

4 Blend together the remaining ingredients and pour over the noodles and vegetables.

5 Stir-fry until thoroughly heated and serve.

FOR A HOTTER FLAVOUR

For a spicy hot chow mein, add 1 tablespoon chilli sauce or substitute chilli oil for the sesame oil.

SPECIAL FRIED RICE

*In this simple recipe, cooked rice is fried with vegetables and cashew
nuts. It can either be eaten on its own or served as an accompaniment.*

STEP 2

SERVES 2–4

*175 g/6 oz/generous ¾ cup long-grain rice
60 g/2 oz/½ cup cashew nuts
1 carrot
½ cucumber
1 yellow (bell) pepper
2 spring onions (scallions)
2 tbsp vegetable oil
1 garlic clove, crushed
125 g/4 oz/¾ cup frozen peas, defrosted
1 tbsp soy sauce
1 tsp salt
coriander (cilantro) leaves to garnish*

1 Bring a large pan of water to the
boil. Add the rice and simmer for
15 minutes. Tip the rice into a sieve
(strainer) and rinse; drain thoroughly.

2 Heat a wok or large frying pan
(skillet), add the cashew nuts and
dry-fry until lightly browned. Remove
and set aside.

3 Cut the carrot in half along the
length, then slice thinly into semi-
circles. Halve the cucumber and remove
the seeds, using a teaspoon; dice the
cucumber. Slice the (bell) pepper and
chop the spring onions (scallions).

4 Heat the oil in the wok or large
frying pan (skillet). Add the
prepared vegetables and the garlic. Stir-
fry for 3 minutes. Add the rice, peas, soy
sauce and salt. Continue to stir-fry until
well mixed and thoroughly heated.

5 Stir in the reserved cashew nuts
and serve garnished with coriander
(cilantro) leaves.

STEP 3

STEP 4

LAST-MINUTE MEAL

You can replace any of the vegetables in
this recipe with others suitable for a stir-
fry, and using leftover rice makes this a
perfect last-minute dish.

STEP 4

FRAGRANT STEAMED RICE IN LOTUS LEAVES

The fragrance of the leaves penetrates the rice, giving it a unique taste. Lotus leaves can be bought from specialist Chinese shops. Large cabbage or spinach leaves can be used as a substitute.

STEP 1

STEP 4

STEP 5

STEP 6

SERVES 4

2 lotus leaves
4 Chinese dried mushrooms (if unavailable, use thinly sliced open-cup mushrooms)
175 g/6 oz/generous ¾ cup long-grain rice
1 cinnamon stick
6 cardamom pods
4 cloves
1 tsp salt
2 eggs
1 tbsp vegetable oil
2 spring onions (scallions), chopped
1 tbsp soy sauce
2 tbsp sherry
1 tsp sugar
1 tsp sesame oil

1 Unfold the lotus leaves carefully and cut along the fold to divide each leaf in half. Lay on a large baking sheet and pour over enough hot water to cover. Leave to soak for about 30 minutes or until the leaves have softened.

2 Place the dried mushrooms in a small bowl and cover with warm water. Leave to soak for 20–25 minutes.

3 Cook the rice in plenty of boiling water in a saucepan with the cinnamon stick, cardamom pods, cloves and salt for about 10 minutes – the rice should be partially cooked. Drain thoroughly and remove the cinnamon stick.

4 Beat the eggs lightly. Heat the oil in a wok or frying pan (skillet) and cook the eggs quickly, stirring constantly until set; then remove and set aside.

5 Drain the mushrooms, squeezing out the excess water. Remove the tough centres and chop the mushrooms. Place the drained rice in a bowl. Stir in the mushrooms, cooked egg, spring onions (scallions), soy sauce, sherry, sugar and sesame oil. Season with salt to taste.

6 Drain the lotus leaves and divide the rice mixture into four portions. Place a portion in the centre of each lotus leaf and fold up to form a parcel (package). Place in a steamer, cover and steam over simmering water for 20 minutes. To serve, cut the tops of the lotus leaves open to expose the fragrant rice inside.

STEP 1

STEP 2

STEP 3

STEP 5

SPICY COCONUT RICE WITH GREEN LENTILS

Rice and green lentils are cooked with creamed coconut, lemon grass and curry leaves. This recipe will serve 2 people as a main course or 4 as an accompaniment.

SERVES 2–4

90 g/ 3 oz/ ¹/₃ cup green lentils
250 g/ 8 oz/ generous 1 cup long-grain rice
2 tbsp vegetable oil
1 onion, sliced
2 garlic cloves, crushed
3 curry leaves
1 stalk lemon grass, chopped (if unavailable, use grated rind of ¹/₂ lemon)
1 green chilli, deseeded and chopped
¹/₂ tsp cumin seeds
1¹/₂ tsp salt
90 g/ 3 oz/ ¹/₃ cup creamed coconut
600 ml/ 1 pint/ 2¹/₂ cups hot water
2 tbsp chopped fresh coriander (cilantro)

TO GARNISH:
shredded radishes
shredded cucumber

1 Wash the lentils and place in a saucepan. Cover with cold water, bring to the boil and boil rapidly for 10 minutes. Wash the rice thoroughly and drain well.

2 Heat the oil in a large saucepan, which has a tight-fitting lid, and fry the onion for 3–4 minutes. Add the garlic, curry leaves, lemon grass, chilli, cumin seeds and salt, and stir well.

3 Drain the lentils and rinse. Add to the onion and spices with the rice and mix well. Add the creamed coconut to the hot water and stir until dissolved. Stir into the rice mixture and bring to the boil. Turn down the heat to low, put the lid on tightly and leave to cook undisturbed for 15 minutes.

4 Without removing the lid, remove the pan from the heat and leave to rest for 10 minutes to allow the rice and lentils to finish cooking in their own steam.

5 Stir in the coriander (cilantro) and remove the curry leaves. Serve garnished with shredded radishes and cucumber.

CREAMED COCONUT

If creamed coconut is unavailable, use 60 g/2 oz/²/₃ cup desiccated (shredded) coconut. Infuse it in the hot water for 20 minutes, drain well and squeeze out any excess water. Discard the coconut and use the liquid.

STEP 2

STEP 3

STEP 5

STEP 6

EGG FU-YUNG WITH RICE

In this dish, cooked rice is mixed with scrambled eggs, Chinese mushrooms, bamboo shoots and water chestnuts, and it is a great way of using up leftover cooked rice. It can be served as a meal by itself or as an accompaniment.

SERVES 2–4

175 g/6 oz/generous ³/₄ cup long-grain rice
2 Chinese dried mushrooms (if unavailable, use thinly sliced open-cup mushrooms)
3 eggs, beaten
3 tbsp vegetable oil
4 spring onions (scallions), sliced
¹/₂ green (bell) pepper, chopped
60 g/2 oz/¹/₃ cup canned bamboo shoots
60 g/2 oz/¹/₃ cup canned water chestnuts, sliced
125 g/4 oz/2 cups bean-sprouts
2 tbsp light soy sauce
2 tbsp dry sherry
2 tsp sesame oil
salt and pepper

1 Cook the rice in lightly salted boiling water according to the packet instructions.

2 Place the dried mushrooms in a small bowl, cover with warm water and leave to soak for 20–25 minutes.

3 Mix the beaten eggs with a little salt. Heat 1 tablespoon of the oil in a wok or large frying pan (skillet). Add the eggs and stir until just set. Remove and set aside.

4 Drain the mushrooms and squeeze out the excess water. Remove the tough centres and chop the mushrooms.

5 Heat the remaining oil in a clean wok or frying pan (skillet). Add the mushrooms, spring onions (scallions) and green (bell) pepper, and stir-fry for 2 minutes. Add the bamboo shoots, water chestnuts and bean-sprouts. Stir-fry for 1 minute.

6 Drain the rice thoroughly and add to the pan with the remaining ingredients. Mix well, heating the rice thoroughly. Season to taste with salt and pepper. Stir in the reserved eggs and serve.

WASHING BEAN-SPROUTS

To wash bean-sprouts, place them in a bowl of cold water and swirl with your hand. Remove any long tail ends.

CHINESE COOKING

SPECIAL INGREDIENTS

Here are a few of the ingredients commonly used in Chinese cooking. They are becoming widely available, particularly in larger supermarkets and health-food stores, but substitutes can be used for the more unusual items.

Bamboo shoots

First growth of the bamboo plant, cut just as it emerges from the ground. The tender shoots are crisp and ivory-coloured with a slightly sweet taste. They are available sliced in cans. Store them in a small bowl in the refrigerator, covered with cold water which should be changed daily. They will keep for up to 7 days.

Bean-sprouts

Grown from mung or soya beans, these are available fresh, canned or in jars. They have a crunchy texture.

Black beans

Salted fermented soya beans, available in packets or cans.

Chillies

These can be red or green, and come in a variety of sizes – the smaller the chilli, the hotter it is, and dried chillies are hotter than fresh. Take care when handling them, as chilli juice stings; avoid touching your eyes and always wash your hands thoroughly afterwards. Discard the seeds, as these are the hottest part.

THE CHINESE DIET

The daily diet of the Chinese is one of the healthiest in the world. Being such a vast country, China encompasses a number of different climates, which gives rise to a wide variety of produce. In addition, the selection of vegetables available in the markets has increased in recent years as China's peasants have been encouraged to grow and sell their own crops.

The vegetarian element

Widespread poverty means that many people are unable to afford meat, and many follow a vegetarian diet for religious reasons. But even when they have the choice, the Chinese have many reasons for eating a largely vegetarian diet. They recognize that a mostly vegetarian diet is the healthiest way to eat, and base their diet on vegetables and carbohydrates (such as rice or noodles), with only a little fish or meat added for flavour. In addition, it is more economical to use the land for growing vegetables and rice than for grazing livestock, as the crops will feed far more people than the livestock will – a crucial factor, considering China's huge and increasing population.

EATING THE CHINESE WAY

Chinese cooking is one of the oldest known cuisines, and its influence has spread throughout the world. The secret of Chinese cooking lies in the art of combining ingredients to give a harmonized contrast in flavour, colour and texture. The recipes in this book have been designed to do just that. They are quick and simple to prepare and they mostly use ingredients obtained from supermarkets. Occasionally you may need to visit a Chinese food store to find one or two ingredients. Some of the recipes have been adapted for the vegetarian from traditional Chinese recipes, and others are vegetarian dishes that have been developed to suit the Western kitchen.

Meal times in China are often family gatherings, at which many different dishes are served. A wide range of ingredients is used, but the different flavours of the many dishes are always made to work together. The meal is served all at once, including the soup. Unlike the Western convention, the Chinese never serve an individual dish to each person; all the dishes on the table are shared.

Preparing a Chinese meal

When planning a menu for this kind of shared meal, allow one dish per person. For example, if you are cooking for only two or three people, serve one main dish with one vegetable side dish and one rice or noodle dish, plus a soup if desired. For an informal meal for four to six people, serve four dishes plus soup and rice; for a formal dinner allow six to eight dishes. Always increase the number of dishes rather than the quantity of ingredients when cooking for many people, as this will give more variety on the table.

Do not choose too many dishes that need a lot of last-minute preparation or have to be served immediately, such as stir-fries. Vary the dishes so that some may be prepared in advance, and then you too can enjoy the meal and not spend all evening in the kitchen.

Preparing to cook

Chinese food generally takes much longer to prepare than it does to cook, so it is very important to prepare each dish as much in advance as possible. Have all the vegetables chopped and sauces blended before you start cooking.

The ingredients should be cut into small, uniformly sized pieces. This ensures that the food will cook evenly. The prepared food is often cooked very briefly over a high heat, which seals in the natural juices and helps to preserve the nutrients. This short cooking time leaves the end product more succulent and preserves its texture as well as its natural flavours and colours. Thinly shredding vegetables and slicing them diagonally ensures fast cooking, as it increases the area that comes into contact with the hot oil.

COOKING METHODS AND EQUIPMENT

It can be very easy to cook Chinese-style in a Western kitchen, and it is not essential to have a collection of exotic cooking utensils. Below are explanations of the methods and equipment most commonly used in Chinese cooking.

Stir-frying

This is the method of cooking most commonly associated with Chinese cooking. The correct piece of equipment for this is a wok, although any large frying pan (skillet) or heavy saucepan will do. The wok is a large sloping-sided heavy metal pan with a rounded bottom. Nowadays it is usually made from carbon iron and has attached to it one or two metal or wooden handles.

Stir-frying with a wok is a very healthy way to cook, as it uses very little oil and preserves the nutrients in the food as they cook for such a short time. It is very important that the wok is very hot before you begin to cook. This can be tested by holding your hand flat 7.5cm/3 inches over the base of the interior, when you will feel the heat radiating from it. The success of stir-frying lies in having the wok at the right temperature, and correct timing when cooking the food.

Add a small amount of oil to the wok and heat it, then add, in stages, the various ingredients to be cooked – those requiring longer cooking go in first, while those that require only very little cooking go in last. The ingredients should be stirred constantly for a very short time using a long-handled metal or wooden spoon or flat scoop. Constantly stirring ensures that all the ingredients come into contact with the hot oil so the natural juices of the food are sealed in, leaving it crisp and colourful. It also ensures that all the ingredients are evenly cooked. Stir-fried dishes are best served immediately.

Clean the wok after each use by washing it with water, using a mild detergent if necessary, and a soft cloth or brush. Do not scrub or use any abrasive cleaner as this will scratch the surface.

Chilli oil

A very hot oil flavoured by chillies and red in colour; use sparingly. You can make your own by adding a few dried chillies to some oil and leaving them to soak for a few days to allow the flavour to come out.

Chinese dried mushrooms

Add flavour and a distinctive aroma. Sold dried in packets and can be expensive, but only a few are needed per dish and they store indefinitely. Soak in warm water for 20 minutes, squeeze dry and discard the stalks. Use open-cup mushrooms as a substitute.

Chinese leaves

Now widely available, these look like a pale, elongated head of lettuce with light green, tightly packed crinkly leaves.

Coriander (cilantro)

Also known as Chinese parsley. The pretty leaves make a very good garnish as well as adding a distinctive flavour to the dish.

Five-spice powder

An aromatic seasoning made from a blend of five spices: star anise, fennel seed, cloves, cinnamon and Sichuan pepper.

Ginger root

A knobbly root that is peeled before use. Use chopped, sliced or grated. It will keep for several weeks in a cool dry place. Can also be kept frozen – break off lumps as needed.

Lemon grass
An aromatic herb, available as fresh stems or dried as serai powder. Chop or slice the lower part of the stem to use.

Lily flowers
Also known as Golden Needles, these are dried lily-flower buds. Soak in water before use.

Lotus leaves
Leaves of the lotus plant. They are very large and sold dried. Soak in hot water before use. These are often used as a shell in which other ingredients are cooked, such as steamed rice.

Noodles
Made from rice, pulses or wheat. There is a large variety available, all of which can be interchanged in recipes. Cook according to packet instructions as times vary from one type to another.

Rice vinegar
A light delicate vinegar made from rice. White wine vinegar can be used in its place.

Sesame seeds
Add texture and a nutty flavour. Dry-fry to add colour and accentuate the flavour.

Soy sauce
Made from fermented soya beans. Widely used and is the main flavouring in Chinese cooking. It is dark or light, the light having a more delicate flavour than the dark.

Dry thoroughly with paper towels or over a low heat, then wipe the surface all over with a little oil. This forms a protective layer from moisture and helps to prevent the wok from rusting.

Steaming

This is another very popular Chinese method of cooking. The piece of equipment the Chinese use is a bamboo steamer. As these are not airtight, they allow a certain amount of steam to escape, preventing any condensation from forming on the lid. They are designed to stand one on top of another, enabling you to cook several dishes at the same time. Bamboo steamers can be bought at Chinese speciality shops or good cookware shops in a range of sizes.

There are two methods of steaming; in the first the food is arranged on a plate or bowl which is then put inside a steamer on the perforated rack and placed over a large pot of boiling water or put inside a wok. The steam passes through the steamer and cooks the food. Larger items of food such as dumplings can be placed straight on to the rack or laid on cabbage or soaked lotus leaves, which prevents the food from falling through and adds extra flavour. Alternatively, the bowl of ingredients can be immersed partway into the boiling water and the food is cooked partly by the boiling water and partly by the steam it produces.

Deep-frying

Use either a wok, a deep-fryer or a heavy-based saucepan. When deep-frying in a wok, use enough oil to give a depth of about 5 cm/2 inches and heat it over a moderate heat until you can see a faint haze of smoke rising before gently lowering in the food to be fried. Make sure the oil is up to temperature before adding the food; the hot oil should cook the food quickly on the outside, sealing it and forming a barrier around it, which prevents the food from acting like a sponge and becoming soggy and greasy, which is what will happen if the oil is not hot enough.

Cook the food in small batches so as not to overcrowd the wok or pan, as this can reduce the temperature of the oil, and lead to unevenly cooked food. Always remove the food from the oil with a perforated spoon and drain on paper towels, to absorb any excess oil.

Braising

This method is very similar to Western braising. Stir-fry the ingredients, then add stock and cook over a low heat. Thicken the sauce at the end of cooking.

Chopsticks

These are long wooden or plastic sticks used not only for eating but also for cooking, as they can be used to stir, whip and beat the food. They can be bought in most cookshops and from many Chinese restaurants.

GARNISHES

Chinese food should always be pleasing to the eye as well as the palate. The dishes can be intricately decorated with delicately cut vegetables, adding colour as well as a finishing touch. The garnishes can be as simple or elaborate as you wish, depending on time and patience. The more simple garnishes could be sprigs of fresh herbs or chopped herbs such as coriander (cilantro), chervil or chives, thin shreds of spring onion (scallion), chilli, lemon zest, slices of radish, or twists of lime or lemon slices.

Spring onion (scallion) brushes

Trim the green top and remove the white part. Shred the green end finely, leaving 2.5 cm/1 inch intact. Place in iced water until the cut end opens out and curls. This can also be done for short lengths of celery and chillies, cutting the end opposite the stalk.

Radishes

For radish roses, trim the ends, then hold the knife flat to the radish skin and make short vertical cuts around the sides, as if you were shaving off the outer skin, but without detaching each 'petal'. Plunge straight into iced water to open out.

Carrot flowers

Peel the carrot. Using a sharp knife make about 5 or 6 tiny V-shaped cuts along the length of the carrot. Then cut into slices: the V-shapes will ensure each slice looks like a flower.

Cucumber

Cut a piece of cucumber about 2.5 cm/ 1 inch long and divide this in half lengthways. Lay a piece of cucumber cut side down and, using a small, sharp knife, cut thin slices along the length to within 1 cm/½ inch of the end. Carefully turn alternate slices over in half and tuck in. Place the pieces in iced water until required.

Tomatoes

For tomato roses peel off the skin of a tomato using a sharp knife in one long strip. Curl the skin into a circle.

ADDED EXTRAS

In addition to the staple ingredients shown in this section, there are some delicious Chinese sauces you can add while cooking your dish, or just before serving it, which will enhance its authentic flavour. Here are a few suggestions:

Bean sauce

Black and yellow bean sauces are used for flavouring dishes or as a condiment. They are both made from ground salted soya beans mixed with flour and spices.

Chilli sauce

A very hot sauce made from chillies, salt and vinegar, usually sold in bottles. Use sparingly – you can always add more if the taste is too mild. Tabasco sauce can be used as a substitute.

Hoisin sauce

Also known as barbecue sauce, this is made from soya beans and seasonings. It is sold in jars ready made and will keep for several months in the refrigerator after it has been opened.

Sesame seed oil

Sesame seed oil has a strong flavour and is used for flavouring rather than for frying, particularly as it tends to burn. Add in small quantities to salad dressings and sauces, or sprinkle lightly over food before serving.

Straw mushrooms

These small, smooth, oval-shaped mushrooms are available in cans. Button mushrooms can be used as a substitute.

Tofu (beancurd)

Made from puréed soya beans, this is white, with a soft cheese-like texture, and is sold in blocks, either fresh or vacuum-packed. It is high in protein and low in fat which makes it an invaluable vegetarian food. Although it has a bland flavour, it blends well with other ingredients, and absorbs the flavours of spices and sauces. It is also available smoked.

Water chestnuts

These are available fresh or in cans. White with a crunchy texture, they will keep in the refrigerator in a small bowl covered in water for up to 7 days, if you change the water each day. These are particularly good for adding texture to stir-fries.

Wonton skins or wrappers

These are made from flour, egg and water. They can be deep-fried on their own and served with a dipping sauce or filled then deep fried, steamed or boiled. Buy them ready-made or make your own (see page 22). Layers of filo pastry make a reasonable substitute. They can be kept frozen for up to 6 months.

INDEX